THE

ELIZABETHAN

CLUB

SERIES

I

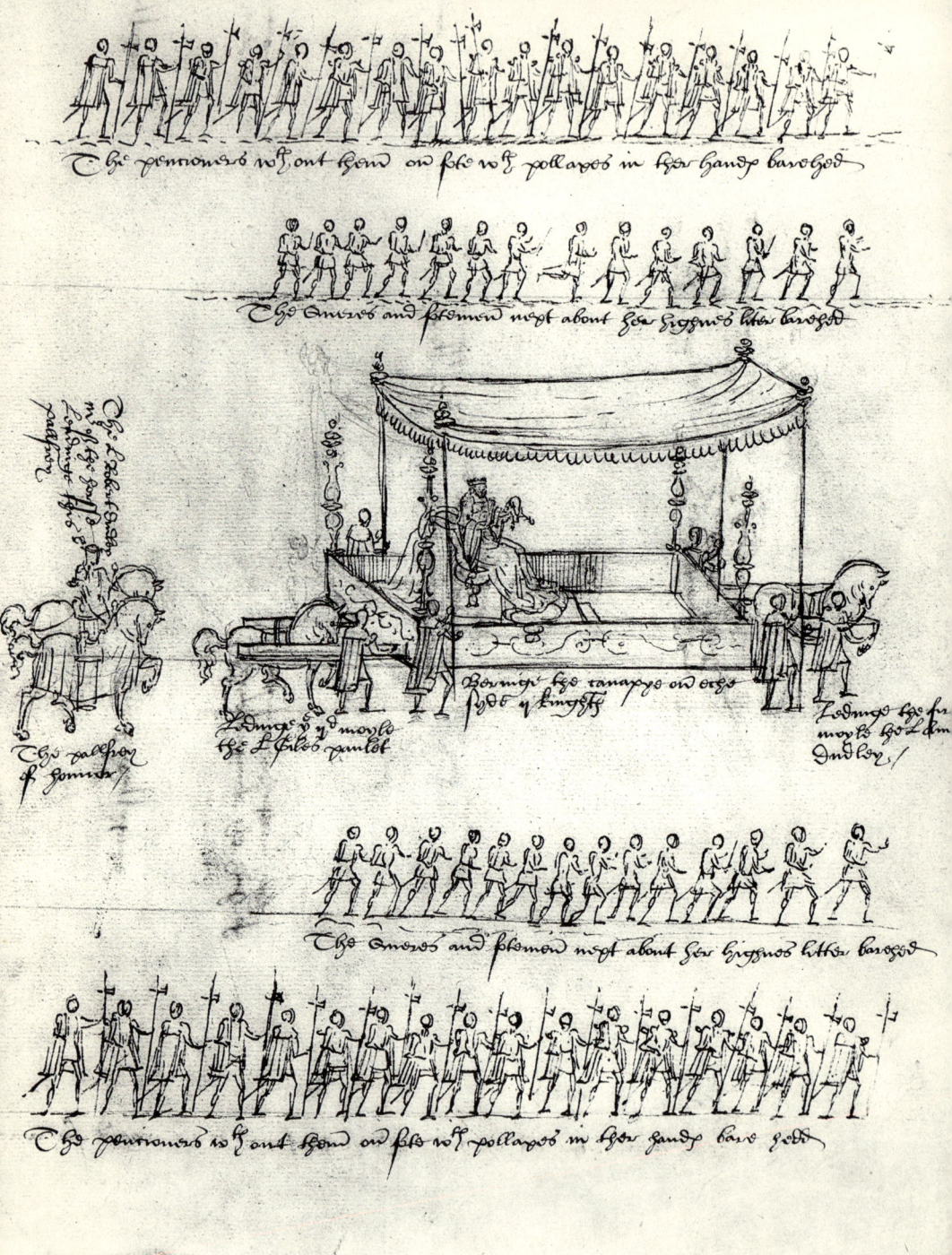

Reproduced from Egerton MS 3320, by courtesy of the Trustees of the British Museum. The drawing depicts the Queen in her litter on the way from Whitehall to her coronation at Westminster. This was on Sunday, January 15, the day following her passage through the City of London; and undoubtedly the same litter was used on both occasions.

The Quenes Maiesties

Passage through the Citie of London

to Westminster

the Day before her Coronacion

edited by James M. Osborn

with an Introduction by
SIR JOHN NEALE

Published for the Elizabethan Club

New Haven, Yale University Press, 1960

© 1960 by *Yale University Press, Inc.*
Printed in the United States of America by
The Meriden Gravure Co., Meriden, Conn.
All rights reserved. This book may not be
reproduced, in whole or in part, in any form
(except by reviewers for the public press),
without written permission from the publishers.
Library of Congress catalog card number: 60-6607

FOREWORD

*T*HE YEAR 1959, the four-hundredth anniversary of the coronation of Queen Elizabeth I, will be remembered as an *annus mirabilis* in the history of the Elizabethan Club at Yale. Ceremonies celebrating the event included a concert of Elizabethan music, a lecture by the Queen's biographer, Sir John Neale, and an exhibition of Elizabethan books, maps, and manuscripts in the University Library. The celebrations culminated in a Solemn Feast notable for its gastronomic gusto and the music especially composed for the occasion by our member, Mr. Quincy Porter.

The year 1959 is memorable for another reason: an agreement was reached with the Yale University Press to publish a series of volumes of Elizabethan interest. Thanks to the Oliver Beattie Cunningham Fund, an annual sum will be available for this purpose.

As the first publication of this series, the present volume is a felicitous choice. Not only is it the first book published about Queen Elizabeth but the Elizabethan Club copy is the only complete copy known of what proves to be the first edition, a fact established during the preparation of this reprint. Happily, Sir John Neale, an honorary member of the Club, was persuaded

Foreword

to write an introduction in which he reveals the book in a new light, as the first piece of Elizabethan propaganda intended to build in the minds of the citizenry the image of Elizabeth as their personal Queen.

The date of publication we have selected is January 14, 1960, exactly four hundred and one years after the pageantry described in the following pages.

Publications Committee of
The Elizabethan Club
    JAMES M. OSBORN, *Chairman*
    LOUIS L. MARTZ
    EUGENE M. WAITH

INTRODUCTION

*I*T HAD long been customary for the Kings of England to lodge for a night or more in the Tower of London and from there to start their coronation procession through the streets of the city to Westminster; though, as neither time nor human endurance permitted both coronation and procession to take place on one day, the elaborate and lengthy ceremonies of the coronation were usually timed for the day after the procession. Chroniclers and others record the events of both these spectacular days for the four coronations of the sixteenth century; and, if their accounts can be relied on, the city procession became increasingly important until, with Queen Elizabeth, it was finally transformed from an introit to the coronation into an occasion in its own right—a popular and secular companion for the subsequent solemn sacrament, worthy of commemoration, as commemorated it was, in print. *The Quenes Maiesties Passage through the Citie of London to Westminster*, with its description of the "pageants" along the route and its picture of Queen and citizens courting one another with delightful ardour, is a fascinating little volume, and, in its way, a most remarkable one. Happy indeed was the thought that prompted the Elizabethan Club of Yale Univer-

Introduction

sity to reproduce their copy of the volume as a final salute to the fourth centenary of an outstanding historical occasion.

The chronicler Hall has left us a description of Henry VIII's coronation procession. There were no "pageants." The spectacle was confined to the impressive and glamorous train of the King and his Queen, Catherine, passing through streets hung with tapestry and cloth of arras and lined with citizens, marshalled in their crafts behind protective rails. A group of "virgins in white, with branches of white wax" was as near as they came to the later notion of a pageant. Edward VI's procession does not seem to have differed much from his father's. Indeed, the Imperial ambassador, a member of the royal *cortège* and perhaps familiar with more elaborate spectacles abroad, reported that there was "no very memorable show of triumph or magnificence." He, however, was an ailing man, and obviously the snail-like progress of the procession—"we were quite four hours on the way from the Tower to Westminster," he says—stirred no enthusiasm in him. He did not deign to notice the diversion recorded by the chronicler Stow at St. Paul's, where a foreign tightrope walker gave a breath-taking display on a rope descending from the steeple of the church.

Introduction

Holinshed, in his description, adds a vague remark about "pageants in divers places, erected to testify the good wills of the citizens"; but one suspects that he invented the passage, misled by our little Elizabethan volume—which is reprinted in his *Chronicles*—into thinking that such pageants had a long history.

Pageants, in the Elizabethan pattern, seem to have begun with Mary Tudor's coronation procession. Honest John Stow tells of them:

> At Fenchurch was a costly pageant made by the Genoese; at Gracechurch corner there was another pageant, made by the Easterlings. At the upper end of Grace Street there was another pageant made by the Florentines, very high; on the top whereof there stood four pictures, and in the midst of them and most highest, there stood an angel all in green, with a trumpet in his hand, and when the trumpeter, who stood secretly in the pageant, did sound his trump, the angel did put his trump in his mouth, as though it had been the same that had sounded, to the great marvelling of many ignorant persons: this pageant was made with three thoroughfares or gates. The conduit in Cornhill ran wine, and

Introduction

beneath the conduit a pageant, made at the charges of the city, and another at the great conduit in Cheap, and a fountain by it running wine. The standard in Cheap new painted, with the waits of the city aloft thereof playing. The cross in Cheap new washed and burnished. One other pageant at the little conduit in Cheap, next to Paul's, made by the city, where the aldermen stood.

Here the Recorder made a short "proposition" or oration, and the Chamberlain presented the Queen with a purse of cloth of gold, containing 1,000 marks of gold. In Paul's churchyard, against the school, Master Heywood—John Heywood, the epigrammatist—sat in a pageant under a vine and made an oration to the Queen in Latin and English, while Peter, a Dutchman, emulated the tight-rope display of Edward VI's procession. There were further pageants against the Dean of Paul's gate and at the conduit in Fleet Street.

How like the display for Queen Elizabeth! And yet how unlike! The main pageants, we notice, were the handiwork of the foreign communities in London. In fact, a foreign commentator sums up the shows in these words: "On

Introduction

the streets were several arches, but only two of them worth noticing, one by the Genoese, the other by the Florentines." His description of these reveals that the Florentine arch or pageant had statues of the principal Virtues and a Fame, with appropriate verses: a conceit that was to be borrowed, and far excelled, in 1559.

It looks very much as if the introduction of pageants into the coronation procession was a foreign importation, perhaps from Italy. Certainly, the outstanding Marian pageants were foreign. This is a fact which brings out for us the significance that a passage in our Elizabethan pamphlet must have had for its readers in 1559: "Thus the Queen's Highness passed through the city, which, without any foreign person, of itself beautified itself." Even the foreign tight-rope walker of Paul's, who had appeared in Edward VI's, as well as Mary's, procession, was omitted from Queen Elizabeth's; and in his place a child from St. Paul's school delivered an oration in Latin, comparing Elizabeth with Plato's philosopher-king.

Londoners, who had demonstrated time and again in Philip and Mary's reign their dislike of that foreign-tinged regime, were determined to assert their native Englishry as a symbol of the new era. Their mood was in tune with their

Introduction

young Queen, who boasted of being "mere English." She had already countered the patronage of Spanish Philip's special ambassador by telling him that it was "the people," and not his master, who "had placed her where she now is." "She is very much attached to the people," he reported, "and very confident that they take her part: which," he added, "is true." How true, this pamphlet of ours reveals; as, indeed, does the whole story of her life and reign.

Their Englishry was only half of London's message for Elizabeth. The city was a hotbed of religious radicalism, and its people, generally speaking, were tired of five years of priestly rule. The fires of Smithfield, as well as the Spanish complexion of the reign, culminating in the profound humiliation of losing Calais in King Philip's war, had united both religious zealots and ordinary folk in a common longing for a return to Protestantism. Though he wrote nearly two decades later, Holinshed ends his account of Mary Tudor's reign with words that voice the mood of Londoners in November 1558: "Thus far the troublesome reign of Queen Mary the first of that name; God grant she may be the last of her religion."

For most Londoners, Elizabeth had long been their "very present help in trouble"; and into

Introduction

their pageants on January 14, 1559, they put the yearnings of their hearts. These were not mere diversions or spectacles, striking and successful though they were as such. In unmistakable language, verbal, pictorial, and symbolical, they proclaimed the new, revolutionary England which the citizens confidently expected her to inaugurate. In the thoughts of such Englishmen Elizabeth, even before her accession, had been their Deborah; and now, in their fifth and last pageant, the city portrayed that biblical ruler, "the judge and restorer of the house of Israel," sitting with her estates as a Queen, "richly apparelled in parliament robes, with a sceptre in her hand." We may smile at the anachronism, but how prophetic the vision! For is it not in her parliaments that we today see the supreme setting of the historic Queen Elizabeth? And how prophetic, also, were the verses attached to that pageant, recording that Deborah "judged Israel till forty years were past"!

The City had given long thought and great pains to its part in the memorable day. What it could not plan, nor perhaps foresee, was the instinctive genius of their young heroine, whose spontaneous and unconventional reactions to everything and everyone converted London on that day into what the author of our pamphlet

Introduction

describes as "a stage wherein was shewed the wonderful spectacle of a noble-hearted Princess toward her most loving people, and the people's exceeding comfort in beholding so worthy a Sovereign, and hearing so princelike a voice." A Mantuan envoy thought "she exceeded the bounds of gravity and decorum." Not so Londoners, nor, indeed, any modern reader of our pamphlet.

The coronation procession took place on January 14, 1559. *The Quenes Maiesties Passage* bears, as the date of imprint, January 23; and it is obvious that the Mantuan envoy, Il Schifanoya, whose dispatch describing the procession is dated that same day, must have had a copy of the pamphlet by him when writing the letter. Quick work! In all probability it was no mere journalistic or publisher's venture but propaganda for the new regime. As such, the pamphlet has additional interest, being the first of innumerable items in the fascinating but unwritten history of official propaganda during Elizabeth's reign.

Propaganda is a main weapon in the armoury of revolution, and it had been exploited by English Protestants both at home and abroad during Mary's reign. Sir William Cecil was—or at any rate, became—a great believer in it. Whether

Introduction

he had anything to do with the composition of our pamphlet may perhaps be doubted. The style is too warm-blooded: certainly, he could not have written it. The Queen herself was even more alive to the value of propaganda than Cecil; and the extent to which she had a part in this activity of her reign has yet to be fully discovered. Though there can be no suspicion that she herself wrote the pamphlet, or even supervised the production—for in that event she would have left her highly sophisticated mark upon its style—she would have approved both the idea and its execution. What can be said with assurance is that the passages concerning the Queen's unrehearsed actions and remarks must have come from someone close to her throughout the procession; and he must have been statesman or courtier. This strengthens the suggestion that the pamphlet was officially inspired: which is far from implying that it is untrue either in fact or in atmosphere. But who the gifted author was seems beyond speculation—save that he may have been one of the Marian exiles, returned to his homeland to share in the building of the New Jerusalem.

J. E. NEALE

BIBLIOGRAPHICAL NOTE

*T*WO EDITIONS of this little book appeared on or soon after January 23, 1559. (Both bear the date 1558 on the title page, as the New Year did not then officially begin until March 25.) The edition here reproduced is the copy that has long been one of the treasures of the Elizabethan Club.

The *Short Title Catalogue* lists only this copy of *The Quenes Maiesties Passage* (STC 7591); this edition was unrecorded in bibliographical history before 1890, when it was displayed in Quaritch's American Exhibition. In 1892 Quaritch's Catalogue No. 124 offered the volume as lot 477, priced at £52.10.0. Doubtless it passed through several hands before Mr. Alexander Smith Cochran presented it as part of his munificent gift of books when the Elizabethan Club was founded in 1911.

The other edition has a longer title, which reads THE *PASSAGE* / *of our most drad Soueraigne Lady* / *Quene Elyzabeth through the* / *citie of London to Westmin-*/ *ster the day before her* / *coronacion.* Of this edition (STC 7590) the editors of the forthcoming revision, Messrs. W. A. Jackson and F. S. Ferguson, report that five copies are known: they are in the British Museum, the Bodleian, Westminster Abbey, Lam-

Bibliographical Note

beth Palace, and the copy preserved by Horace Walpole, now at the Huntington Library in California. Another copy, lacking the title page, has been found in the Guildhall Library.[1]

These two editions are very similar in appearance; both consist of five sheets, each of eight pages (A–E^4). Comparison promptly reveals that one edition was deliberately prepared as a facsimile of the other, being a page-by-page, line-by-line reprint. The only obvious difference is in the title, though even here the last three lines may have been the exact type used in both editions. The ornamental title-page border appears in both editions, and the same ornamental capital initial was employed on the first page of both.

The problem is to determine which of the two editions came first. Solution depends on the minute examination of a great many textual differences, for all but four pages can be shown to have been reset, and the headings at the top of the pages have usually been shifted slightly to one side or the other. In fact the compositor

---

1. Each leaf of this copy has been mounted and inset on a separate page. Sheets C and D appear to belong to the 7590 edition and Sheet E to 7591. The Guildhall Librarian, Mr. A. H. Hall, suggests "it could be a made-up copy from more than one edition."

Bibliographical Note

of most of the pages has followed his model with unusual care. Only one side of one sheet (the inner form of sheet C—pages Ci verso, Cii recto, Ciii verso and Ciiii recto) has the same setting of type, and here the running heads differ.

The hundreds of textual differences may be divided into two groups, "accidentals" and "substantives." Accidentals are slight changes which do not affect the meaning, but show that the type has been reset (for example, "Quenes" in place of "Queenes", or "woorthye" for Woorthie"). Substantives are changes that do affect the meaning, such as omissions, additions, or substitutions of one word for another. In these two editions the accidentals provide little basis for arguing the priority of one printing over the other, for most of the arguments can be reversed to support the rival point of view. But the substantives provide grounds for believing that the edition owned by the Elizabethan Club (and here reprinted) is the earlier one, from which the other was derived.

To ascertain the substantive differences the Elizabethan Club copy (called Y) has been compared with the Huntington Library copy of the other edition (called Hn). Because the pages are unnumbered, it is necessary to refer

Bibliographical Note

to the signatures placed by the printer at the foot of each leaf.

1. On page Cii of Y the name "sir John Parrat" was wrongly printed; it has been corrected by pasting over his Christian name a slip of paper reading "John". In Hn the name has been correctly printed.

2. Similarly, on page Ciiii copy Y reads "maister Parrat", whereas in Hn his title is correctly given as Sir John. (No problem of chronology exists, for Perrot had been created a Knight of the Bath by King Edward VI several years earlier.)

3. In Y, signature Cii is wrongly printed as Ciii, whereas in copy Hn it is correctly given.

4. In the bottom line on Eiii copy Y reads "al natural Englishmen"; Hn reads "all Englishemen", thereby dropping out an important word which, if Hn were earlier, the printer of Y would not have inserted on his own.

5. In several places the compositor of Hn has been careless; for example, he has given two extra lines of verse at the bottom of page Bii, taking them from the top of the following page. He did not come out even again until he reached the bottom of the second page following. Similarly, in signature D the compositor went off again, and added two and a half lines at the

Bibliographical Note

bottom of Di, where he gave all nine "Causes", but in a different order; he carried this difference along on Di verso and finally caught up at the bottom of Dii. But in the process he squeezed the text into 26 lines (Y has 27) which could be managed only by excessive use of contractions, employing three in the bottom line alone. This carelessness argues that copy Hn follows Y, for the compositor of the first edition would not have needed to force his type into any such pattern.

In the absence of positive evidence to the contrary, any one of these examples would be enough to establish that the Elizabethan Club edition preceded the other. This conclusion is supported by the original entry in the Stationers Register, which reads: "Rycharde tottle ys lycensed to prynte *the passage of the quenes maiesties Throwoute the Cytie of London*" (Arber, *Transcript, I*, 96).

How may we then reconstruct the scene in Richard Tottel's printing shop at the sign of the Hand and Star, in January of 1558/9? The surviving evidence suggests that his handsome black-letter printing of *The Quenes Maiesties Passage through the Citie of London to Westminster the Day before her Coronacion* sold like hot cakes, and Tottel set the presses hurriedly to

Bibliographical Note

work on a new edition, an imitation of the first edition as close as his workmen could make it. By chance, type of the four pages comprising the inner form of sheet C was still standing, but the other pages had to be reset. Probably the press run on the second edition was larger than the first, and sale was helped along by the catchy new title, with its high-sounding salute to "our most drad Soueraigne Lady Quene Elyzabeth."

JAMES M. OSBORN

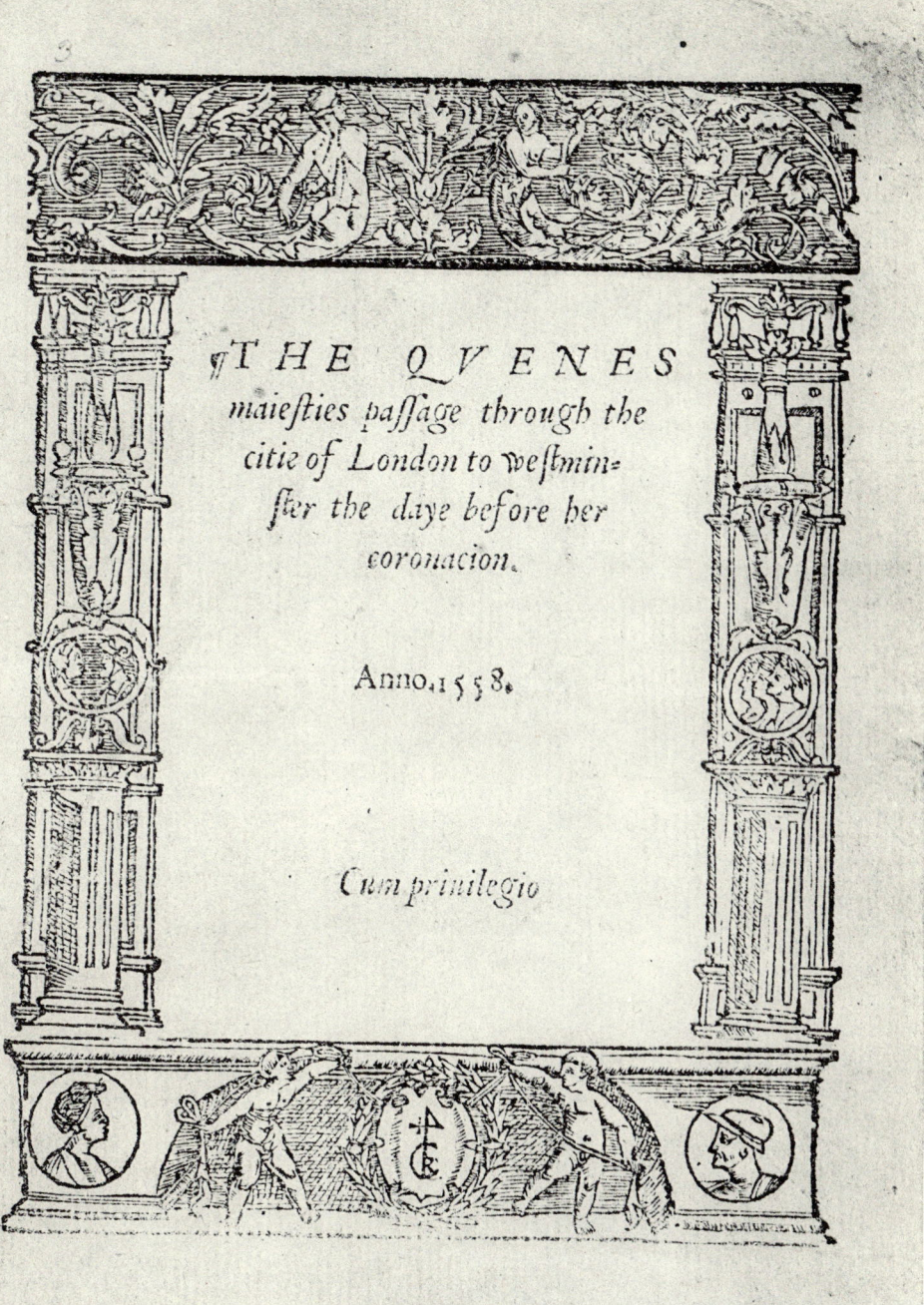

¶THE QVENES
maiesties passage through the
citie of London to westmin=
ster the daye before her
coronacion.

Anno.1558.

Cum priuilegio

The receiuing of the Quenes maiestie.

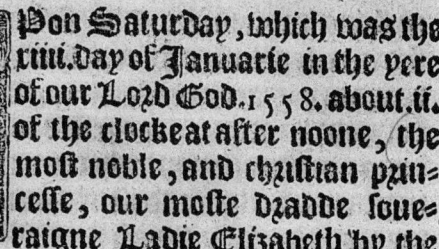Pon Saturday, which was the xiiii. day of Ianuarie in the yere of our Lord God. 1558. about. ii. of the clocke at after noone, the most noble, and christian princesse, our moste dradde soueraigne Ladie Elizabeth by the grace of god Queen of England, Fraunce & Ireland, defendour of the faythe &c. marched from the towre to passe through the citie of London towarde Westminster, richely furnished, & most honorablye accompanied, as wel with gētlemen, Barons, and other the nobilitie of thys realme, as also with a notable trayne of goodly and beawtiful ladies, richely appoynted. And entring the citie was of the people receiued merueylous entierly, as appeared by thassemblie, prayers, wisshes, welcomminges, cryes, tender woordes, and all other signes, whiche argue a wonderfull earnest loue of most obedient subiectes towarde theyr soueraygne. And on thother syde her grace by holding vp her handes, and merie countenaunce to such as stoode farre of, and most tender & gētle language to those that stode nigh to her grace, did declare her selfe no lesse thankefullye to receiue her peoples good wille, than they louingly offred it vnto her. To all that wisshed her grace wel, she gaue heartie thankes, and to suche as bade God saue her grace, she sayd agayne god saue them all, and thanked them with all her heart. So that on eyther syde ther was nothing but gladnes, nothing but prayer,

A.ii. nothing

The receiuing

nothing but comfort. The Quenes maiestie reioysed merueylouslye to see, ÿ so excedingly shewed toward her grace, which all good princes haue euer desyred, I meane so earnest loue of subiectes, so euidently declared euen to her graces own persone being caried in the middest of them. The people again wer wonderfully rauished with the louing answers and gestures of their princesse, like to the which they had before tryed at her first coming to the towre from Hatfield. This her graces louing behauiour preconceiued in the peoples heades vpon these consideracions was then throughly confirmed, and in dede emplanted a woonderfull hope in them touching her woorthie gouernment in the rest of her reygne. For in all her passage she did not only shew her most gracious loue toward the people in generall, but also priuately if the baser personages had either offred her grace any flowres or such like as a significacion of their good will, or moued to her any sute, she most gently, to the common reioysing of all the lookers on, and priuate comfort of ÿ partie, staid her chariot, and heard theyr requestes. So that if a man should say wel, he could not better tearme the citie of London that time, than a stage wherin was shewed the wonderfull spectacle, of a noble hearted princesse toward her most louing people, & the peoples excading comfort in beholding so worthy a soueraign, & hearing so princelike a voice which could not but haue set thenemie on fyre, since ÿ vertue is in ÿ enemie alway comended, much more could not
but

of the Quenes maiestie.

but enflame her naturall, obedient, and most louyng people, whose weale leaneth onely vppon her grace, and her gouernement. Thus therefore the queenes maiestie passed from the Towre tyll she came to Fanchurche, the people on eche syde ioyousyle beholding the viewe of so gracious a Ladie their quene, and her grace no lesse gladlye notyng and obseruynge the same. Nere vnto Fanchurch was erected a scaffold richely furnished, wheron stode a noyes of instrumentes, and a child in costly apparel, which was appointed to welcome the quenes maiestie in ye hole cities behalfe. Against which place when her grace came, of her own wille she comauded the chariot to be staide, & y^t the noyes might be appeased till the child had vttered his welcomming oration, which he spake in English meter as here foloweth.

O pereles soueraygne quene, behold what this thy town
Hath thee presented with at thy fyrst entraunce here:
Behold with how riche hope she ledeth thee to thy crown
Beholde with what two gyftes she comforteth thy chere.
The first is blessing tonges, which many a welcome say
Which pray thou maist do wel, which praise the to ye skie
Which wish to the long lyfe, which blesse this happy day
Which to thy kingdome heapes, all y^t in tonges can lye.
The second is true hertes, which loue thee fro their roote
Whose sute is tryumphe now, and ruleth all the game.
Which faithfulnes haue wone, & al vntruthe disus one,
Which skip for ioy, when as they heare thy happy name.
Welcome therfore O quene, as much as hert can thinke,
Welcome agayn O quene, as much as tong can tell:
Welcome to ioyous tonges, & hertes that wil not shrink,
God thee preserue we praye, & wishe thee euer well.

F.iii. At

The receiuing

At which wordes of ẏ last line the hole peple gaue a great shout, wishing with one assent as the childe had said. And ẏ quenes maiestie thanked most hartely both ẏ citie for this her gētle receiuing at ẏ first, & also ẏ peple for cōfirming ẏ same. Here was noted in the Quenes maiesties coūtenance, during ẏ time that the childe spake, besides a perpetual attētiuenes in her face, a meruelous change in looke, as the childes wordes touched either her persō or the peoples tonges and hertes. So that she with reioysing visage did euidently declare that the woordes tooke no lesse place in her mynde, than they were moste heartelye pronounced by the chylde, as from all the heartes of her most heartie citizeins. The same verses wer fastned vp in a table vpon the scaffolde, and the latine therof likewise in latine verses in another table as hereafter enseweth.

Vrbs tua quæ ingreſſu dederit tibi munera primo,
  O Regina parem non habitura, vide.
Ad diadema tuum, te ſpe quám diuite mittat,
  Quæ duo lætitiæ det tibi dona, vide.
Munus habes primũ, linguas bona multa precātes,
  Quæ te quum laudant, tum pia vota ſonant,
Fœlicemq́, diem huuc dicunt, tibi ſecula longa
  Optant, et quicquid deniq̃ lingua poteſt.
Altera dona feres, vera, et tui amantia corda,
                                   Quorum

of the Quenes maieſtie.

Quorum gens ludum iam regit vna tuum:
In quibus eſt infracta fides, falſumq; peroſa,
Quæq; tuo audito nomine læta ſalit
Grata venis igitur, quantum cor concipit vllum,
Quantum lingua poteſt dicere, grata venis.
Cordibus infractis, linguisq; per omnia lætis
Grata venis: ſaluam te velit eſſe deus.

Now when the childe had pronounced his oration, and the Quenes highnes so thankefully had receiued it, She marched forwarde towarde gracious streate, where at the vpper ende, before the sygne of the Egle, the citie had erected a gorgeous & sumptuous arke as here foloweth.

A stage was made whiche extended from thone syde of the streate to thother, rychelye vawted with batlementes conteining three portes, and ouer the middlemost was auaunced iiii. seuerall stages in degrees. Upon the lowest stage was made one seate royall, wherin wer placed two personages represẽting kynge Henrie the seuenth and Elizabeth hys wyfe daughter of king Edward the fourth, eyther of these two princes sitting vnder one cloth of estate in their seates, no otherwyse diuyded, but that thone of them which was king Henrie the seuenth proceding out of the house of Lancastre, was enclosed in a read rose, and thother which was Queene Elizabeth being heire to the house of Yorke enclosed with

A.iiii.   a whyte

The receiuing

a whyte rose, eche of them royallie crowned, and decently apparailled as apperteineth to prynces, with Sceptours in their hādes, & one bawt surmoūting their heades, wherin aptlie wer placed two tables, eche cōteining ỹ tytle of those two prynces. And these personages wer so set, ỹ the one of them ioyned handes with thother, with ỹ ring of matrimonie perceiued on ỹ finger. Out of the which two roses sprang two brāuches gathered into one, which wer directed vpward to the second stage or degree, wherin was placed one, representing the valiant & noble prynce king Henrie theight which sprong out of the former stocke, crowned w a crowne imperiall, & by him sate one represētīng ỹ right worthie ladie quene Anne, wife to the said king Hērie theyght, & mother to our most soueraign ladie quene Elizabeth that now is, both apparelled with Sceptours & diademes, and other furniture due to the state of a king & quene & ii.tables surmounting their heades, wherein were writtē their names & tytles. Frō their seate also proceaded vpwardes one brāuche directed to the third and vppermost stage or degree, wherin lykewyse was planted a seate royall, in the whiche was sette one representynge the Quenes most excellent maiestie Elizabeth nowe our most dradde soueraygne Ladie, crowned and apparelled as thother prynces were. Oute of the forepart of thys pageaunt was made a standyng for a chylde, whiche at the quenes maiesties comyng declared vnto her ỹ hole meaning of the said pageaunt. The two sydes of the

same

of the Queenes maiestie.

same were filled with loude noyses of musicke. And all emptie places thereof were furnished with sentences concerning vnitie. And the hole pageant garnished with redde roses and white and in the forefront of the same pageant in a faire wreathe was written the name, and title of the same, which was The vniting of the two houses of Lancastre and Yorke. This pageant was grounded vpon the Queenes maiesties name. For like as the long warre betwene the two houses of Yorke and Lancastre then ended, when Elizabeth doughter to Edwarde the fourthe matched in mariage wyth Henry the seuenthe heyre to the howse of Launcaster: so synce that the Queenes maiesties name was Elizabeth, and forsomuch as she is the onelye heire of Henrie the eyght, which came of bothe the houses as the knitting vp of concorde, it was deuised that like as Elizabeth was the first occasion of concorde, so she another Elizabeth might maintaine the same among her subiectes, so that vnitie was the ende wherat the whole deuise shotte, as the Queenes maiesties names moued the firste grounde. This pageant now against the Quenes maiesties comming was addressed with children representing the forenamed personages, with all furniture dew vnto the setting forthe of such a matter well ment, as the argument declared, costly and sumptuouslye set forthe, as the beholders can beare witnes. Now the Queenes maiestye

B.i.

The receiuing

iestye drewe nere vnto the sayde pageant, and forsomuch as the noyse was great by reason of the prease of people, so that she could skace heare the childe which did interprete the saide pageant, and her chariot was passed so farre forward that she could not well view the personages representing the kinges and Queenes abouenamed: she required to haue the matter opened vnto her, which so was, and euery personage appointed, and what they signified, with the ende of vnitie & ground of her name, according as is before expressed. For the sight wherof, her grace caused her chariot to be remoued back, & yet hardly coulde she see, because the children were set somewhat with the farthest in. But after that her grace had vnderstode the meaning therof, she thanked the citie, praised the fairenes of the worke, and promised, that she would doe her whole endeuour for the continuall preseruacion of concorde, as the pageant did emporte. The childe appointed in the standing abouenamed to open the meaning of the said pageant, spake these wordes vnto her grace.

The two princes that sit vnder one cloth of state,
The man in the red rose, the woman in the white:
Henry the .vii. And Queene Elizabeth his mate,
By ryng of mariage as man and wife vnite.

Both heires to both their bloodes, to Lācastre the king
The Queene to Yorke, in one the two houses did knit,
Of whom as heire to both, Henry the eyght did spring,
In whose seat his true heire thou quene Elisabeth dost sit
              Therfore

of the Queenes maiestie.

Therfore as ciuill warre, and shede of blood did cease
When these two houses were vnited into one
So now that iarre shall stint, and quietnes encrease,
We trust, O noble Queene, thou wilt be cause alone.

The which also were written in laten verses,
and bothe drawen in two tables vppon the forefront of the sayde pageant as hereafter foloweth.

Hii quos iungit idem solium quos annulus idem:
  Hæc albente nitens, ille rubente Rosa:
Septimus Henricus Rex, Regina Elizabetha,
  Scilicet Hæredes gentis vterq̃ suæ:
Hæc Eboracensis, Lancastrius ille dederunt
  Connubio, e geminis quo foret vna domus
Excipit hos hæres Henricus copula regum
  Octauus, magni Regis imago potens
Regibus hinc succedis auis, Regiq̃ parenti
  Patris iusta hæres Elizabetha tui.

¶ Sentences placed therin concerning vnite.

Nullæ concordes animos vires domant.
Qui iuncti terrent, deiuncti timent.

B.ii.   *Discordes*

The receiuing

Discordes animi soluunt, concordes ligant.
Augentur parua pace, magna bello cadunt.
Coniunctæ manus fortius tollunt onus.
Regno pro menibus æneis ciuium concordia.
Que diu pugnant diutius lugent.
Dissidentes principes sulditorum lues.
Princeps ad pacem natus non ad arma datur
Filia concordiæ copia, neptis quies.
Dissentiens respublica hostibus placet.
Qui idem tenent, diutius tenent.
Regnum diuisum facile dissoluitur.
Ciuitas concors armis frustra tentatur.
Omnium gentium consensus firmat fidem. &c.

These verses and other pretie sentences were drawen in voide places of this pageant, all tending to one ende that quietnes might be mainteined, and all dissention displaced, and that by the Queenes maiestie, heire to agrement, and agreing in name with her, which tofore had ioyned those houses, which had ben thoccasion of much debate and ciuill warre within this realme, as maye apeare to soche, as will search cronicles, but be not to be touched in this treatise onely declaring her graces passage through the citie, and what prouision the citie made therfore. And ere the Quenes maiestie came within hearing of this pageant, she sent certaine as also at all the other pageants

to

of the Queenes maiestie.

to require the people to be silent for her maiestie was disposed to heare all that shold be said vnto her.

When the Queenes maiestie had hearde the childes oracion, and vnderstode the meaning of the pageant at large, she marched forward toward Cornehill, alway receiued with like reioising of the people, & there as her grace passed by the conduit which was curiouslye trimmed against that time with riche banners adourned, and a noyse of loude instrumentes vpon the top therof, she espied the seconde pageant, and because shee feared for the peoples noyse, that she should not here the child which did expounde thesame, she enquired what that pageant was ere that she came to it. And there vnderstode, that there was a childe representing her maiesties person, placed in a seate of gouernement, supported by certaiue vertues, which suppressed other vices vnder their seate, and so forthe, as in the description of the said pageant shall hereafter apeare.

This pageant standing in the nether ende of Cornehill was extended from thoneside of the strete to the other, and in the same pageant was deuised three gates all open, and ouer the middle parte therof was erected one chaire a seate royall with clothe of estate to the same apperteyning wherein was placed a childe representing the Queenes highnesse with consideracion had for place conuenient for a table which conteined her name and title. And in a comelie wreathe artificiallie

B.iii.

The receiuing

cially and wel deuised with perfite sight and vnder∫tåding to the people. In the fröt of the same pageāt was written the name and title therof, which is The seate of worthie gouernance, which seate was made in such artificiall maner, as to the apperance of the lookers on, the foreparte semed to haue no staie, and therfore of force was stayed by liuely personages, which personages were in numbre foure, standing and staieng the forefront of the same seate royal, eche hauing his face to the Quene and people, wherof euery one had a table to expresse their effectes, which are vertues, namelie Pure religió, Loue of subiectes, VVisedome and Iustice, which did treade their contrarie vices vnder their feete, that is to witte, Pure religion, did treade vppon Superstition, and Ignoraunce, Loue of subiectes, did treade vpon Rebellion and Insolencie, VVisedome did treade vpon follie and vaine glorie, Iustice did treade vpon Adulacion and Briberie. Eche of these personages according to their proper names and properties, had not onlie their names in plaine and perfit writing set vpon their breastes easelie to be read of all, but also euery of them was aptelie and properlie apparelled, so that his apparell and name did agre to expresse the same person, that in title he represented. Thys part of the pageant was thus appointed and furnished. The two sides ouer the two side portes had in them placed a noyse of in∫trumentes, which immediatlie, after the childes speache gaue an heauenly melodie. Upon the top or vpper-

of the Queenes maieſtie.

vppermoſt part of ẏ ſaid pageāt, ſtoode the armes of England roially poztratured with ẏ proper beaſtes to vpholde the ſame. One repreſeting the Quenes highnes ſate in this ſeate crowned with an Imperiall crowne, and before her ſeate, was a conueniēt place appointed for one childe which did interpret and applie the ſaid pageant as hereafter ſhalbe declared. Euery voide place was furniſhed with proper ſentences commending the ſeate ſupported by vertues, and defacing the vices, to the vtter extirpation of rebellion, and to euerlaſting continuance of quietnes and peace. The Queenes maieſtie approching nighe vnto thys pageant thus bewtified and furniſhed in all pointes, cauſed her charyot to be drawen nyghe thereunto, that her grace myght heare the childes oration whych was thys.

While that religion true, ſhall ignorance ſuppreſſe
And with her weightie foote, breake ſuperſtitions heade
While loue of ſubiectes, ſhall rebellion diſtreſſe
And with zeale to the prince, inſolencie down treade.

While iuſtice, can flattering tonges & briberie deface
While follie & vaine glory to wiſedome yelde their hādes
So long ſhal gouernmēt, not ſwarue frō her right race
But wrong decayeth ſtill, and rightwiſenes vp ſtandes.

Now all thy ſubiectes hertes, O prince of perles fame
Do truſt theſe vertues ſhall maintein vp thy throne,
And vice be kept down ſtill, the wicked put to ſhame
That good w̄ good may ioy, & naught w̄ naught may mone

B.iiii. Which

The receiuing

Which verses were painted vpon the right side of the same pageant, and the latin therof on the left side in another table, which were these.

Quæ subnixa alte solio regina superbo est,
 Effigies sanctæ principis alma refert,
Quam ciuilis amor fulcit, sapientia firmat,
 Iusticia illustrat, Relligioq̨ beat.
Vana superstitio et crassæ ignorantia frontis
 Pressæ sub pura relligine iacent.
Regis amor domat effrenes, animosq̨ rebelles
 Iustus adulantes, Domiuorosq̨ terit.
Cum regit imperium sapiens, sine luce sedebunt
 Stulticia, atq̨ huius numen inanis honor.

Beside these verses there were placed in euery voide rome of the pageant both in Englisch and laten such sentences as aduaūced the seate of gouernaunce vpholden by vertue. The grounde of this pageant, was that like as by vertues (which doe aboundantly appere in her grace) the Queenes maiestie was establisched in the seate of gouernement: so she should syt fast in thesame so long as she embraced vertue and helde vice vnder foote. For if vice once gotte vp the head, it woulde put the seate of gouernement in perill of falling. The Queenes maiestie when she had heard the childe and vnderstode the pageant at full, gaue
the

of the Quenes maiestie.

the citie also thankes there, and most graciouslie promised her good endeuour for the maintenance of the sayde vertues, and suppression of vyces, and so marched on till she came against the great conduit in chepe, which was bewtifyed with pictures and sentences accordingly agaynst her graces comming thither.

Against Soper lanes ende was extended from thone syde of the streate to thother, a pageant which had three gates all open. Ouer the middlemoste wherof wer erected three seuerall stages, whereon sate eight childzen as hereafter soloweth. On the vppermost one childe, on the middle three, on the lowest, iiii, eche hauing the proper name of the blessing, that they did represent, written in a table and placed aboue their heades. In the forefront of this pageant before the childzen which did represent the blessinges, was a conuenient standing cast out for a chylde to stande, which did expound the said pageaunt vnto the quenes maiestie, as was done in thother tofore. Euerie of these childzen wer appointed & apparelled according vnto the blessing which he did represent. And on the forepart of the said pageant was written in fayre letters the name of the said pageant in this maner folowing.

The eight beatitudes expressed in the, v. chapter of the gospel of S. Mathew, applyed to our soueraigne Ladie Queene Elizabeth.

Ouer the two side portes was placed a noyes of instrumentes. And all voide places in the pageant

C.i. were

The receiuing

wer furnished with prety sayinges, cōmending and touching ye meaning of the said pageant, which was the promises & blessinges of almightie god made to his people. Before yt the quenes highnes came vnto this pageant, she required ye matter somewhat to be opened vnto her, yt her grace might the better vnderstād, what should afterward by the child be sayd vnto her. Which so was, yt the citie had there erected the pageant with .viii. childꝛen, representing theyght blessinges touched in the .v. Chapiter of S. Mathew. Wherof, euery one vpon iust consideracions was applyed vnto her highnes, and that the people therby put her grace in mind, yt as her good doinges before had geuen iust occasion, why that these blessinges might fall vpon her, yt so if her grace did continue in her goodnes as she had entred, she shoulde hope for the fruit of these promises due vnto them, yt doe exercise themselues in the blessinges, whiche her grace heard merueilous graciously, and required that the chariot myght be remoued towardes the pageaunt, that she might perceyue the chyldes woordes, which were these, the Quenes maiestie geuing most attentiue eare, and requiring that the peoples noyse might be stayde.

Thou hast been .viii. times blest, o quene of worthy fame
By mekenes of thy spirite, when care did thee besette
By mourning in thy griefe, by mildnes in thy blame
By hunger and by thyrst, and iustice couldst none gette.
By mercy shewed, not felt, by cleanes of thyne harte
By sekyng peace alwayes, by persecucion wrong.
Therfore trust thou in god, since he hath helpt thy smart
That as his promis is, so he will make thee strong.

When

of the Quenes maiestie.

When these woordes were spoken, all the people wished, that as the child had spoken, so god woulde strengthen her grace against all her aduersaries, whom ye Quenes maiestie did most gently thanke for their so louing wishe. These verses wer painted on the left syde of the said pageant, and other in laten on thother syde, which wer these.

Qui lugent hilares fient, qui mitia gestant
   Pectora, multa soli iugera culta metent
Iustitiam esuriens sitiensue replebitur, ipsum.
   Fas homini puro corde videre deum
Quē alterius miseret. dominus miserebitur huius,
   Pacificus quisquis, filius ille Dei est.
Propter iustitiam quisquis patietur habetq́,
   Demissam mentem, cælica regna capit.
Huic hominum generi terram, mare, sidera vouit
   Omnipotens, horum quisque beatus erit.

Besides these, euery voide place in ye pageant was furnished with sentences touching the matter and ground of the said pageant. When all ye was to be said in this pageant was ended, the Quenes maiestie passed on forward in Chepe syde.

At the standarde in Cheape which was dressed fayre agaynste the tyme, was placed a noyse of Trumpettes, with banners and other furniture. The Crosse lykewyse was also made fayre and

                C.iii.   well

The receiuing

well trymmed. And neare vnto thesame, vppon the porche of Saint Peters church dore, stode the waites of the citie, which did geue a pleasant noyse with theyr instrumentes as the Quenes maiestie did passe by, which on euerie syde cast her countenaunce, and wished well to all her most louing people. Sone after that her grace passed the crosse, she had espyed the pageant erected at the litle conduit in cheape, and incontinent required to know what it might signifye. And it was tolde her grace, that there was placed Tyme. Tyme: quoth she, and Tyme hath brought me hether. And so furth the hole matter was opened to her grace as hereafter shalbe declared in the descripcion of the pageaunt. But in the openyng, when her grace vnderstoode that the Byble in Englishe shoulde be deliuered vnto her by Truth, whiche was therein represented by a childe: she thanked the citie for that gift, and sayd that she would oftentimes reade ouer that booke, comaunding sir John Parrat, one of the knightes which helde vp her canapy, to goe before and to receiue the booke. But learning that it should be deliuered vnto her grace downe by a silken lace, she caused him to staye, and so passed forward till she came agaynste thaldermen in the hyghe ende of Chepe tofore the little conduite, where the companies of the citie ended, which beganne at Fanchurch, and stoode alonge the streates one by another enclosed with rayles, hanged with clothes, and themselues well apparelled with many ryche

furres

of the Quenes maiestie.

furres and theyr liuery whodes vpon theyr shoulders in comely & semely maner, hauing before thē sondry persones well apparelled in silkes & chaines of golde, as wyflers and garders of the said companies, beside a nūbre of riche hangynges, aswell of Tapistrie, Arras, clothes of golde, siluer, veluet, damaske, Sattyn, and other silkes plentifully hanged all the way as the Quenes highnes passed from the Towre through the citie. Out at the windowes & penthouses of euerie house, did hang a number of ryche and costlye banners and streamers tyll her grace came to the vpper ende of Cheape. And there, by appointment, the right worshipfull maister Ranulph Cholmley Recorder of the citie, presented to the Quenes maiestie a purse of crimosin sattin richly wrought with gold, wherin the citie gaue vnto the Quenes maiestie a thousand markes in gold, as maister Recorder did declare brieflye vnto the Quenes maiestie, whose wordes tended to this ende, that the Lord maior, hys brethren, and comminaltie of the citie, to declare their gladnes and good wille towardes the Quenes maiestie, did present her grace with that gold, desyering her grace to continue their good and gracious Quene, and not to esteme the value of the gift, but the mynd of the geuers. The Quenes maiestie with both her haudes tooke the purse, and aunswered to him againe meruellous pithilie, and so pithilie that the standers by, as they embraced entierly her gracious aunswer, so they mer-

C.iii.　　　uailed

The receceiuing

meruailed at ẏ cowching therof, which was in wordes truely reported these. I thanke my lord maior, his brethren, & you all. And wheras your request is that I should continue your good ladie & quene, be ye ensured, that I wil be as good vnto you, as euer quene was to her people. No wille in me can lacke, neither doe I trust shall ther lacke any power. And perswade your selues, that for the safetie and quietnes of you all, I will not spare, if nede be to spend my blood, God thanke you all. Whiche aunswere of so noble an hearted pryncesse, if it moued a meruaylous showte and reioysing, it is nothyng to be meruayled at, since both the heartines thereof was so woonderfull, and the woordes so ioyntly knytte. When her grace hadde thus aunswered the Recorder, she marched toward the little conduit, where was erected a pageaunt with squaze proportion, standynge directlye before thesame conduite, with battlementes accordyngly. And in thesame pageaunt was aduaunced two hylles or mountaynes of conuenient heyghte. The one of them beyng on the North syde of thesame pageaunt, was made cragged, barreyn, and stonye, in the whiche was erected one tree, artificiallye made, all withered and deadde, with braunches accordinglye. And vnder thesame tree at the foote thereof, sate one in homely and rude apparell crokedlye, and in mournyng maner, hauynge ouer hys headde in a table, written in Latin and Englyshe, hys name, whiche was Ruinosa Respublica, A decayed com=

of the Quenes maieſtie.

ed common weale. And vppon theſame withered tree were fixed certayne Tables, wherein were written proper ſentences, expreſſing the cauſes of the decaye of a common weale. The other hylle on the South ſyde was made fayre, freſhe, grene, and beawtifull, the grounde thereof full of flowres and beawtie, and on theſame was erected alſo one tree very freſhe and fayre, vnder the whiche, ſtoode vprighte one freſhe perſonage well apparaylled and appoynted, whoſe name alſo was written bothe in Englyſhe and in Laten, whiche was, Respublica bene instituta. A floriſhyng common weale. And vppon theſame tree alſo, were fixed certayne Tables conteyning ſentences, which expreſſed the cauſes of a flouriſhing common weale. In the middle betwene the ſayde hylles, was made artificiallye one hollowe place or caue, with doore and locke encloſed, oute of the whiche, a lyttle before the Queenes hyghnes commynge thither, iſſued one perſonage whoſe name was Tyme, apparaylled as an olde man with a Sythe in his hande, hauynge wynges artificiallye made, leadinge a perſonage of leſſer ſtature then himſelfe, whiche was fynely and well apparaylled, all cladde in whyte ſilke, and directlye ouer her head was ſet her name and tytle in latin and Englyſhe, Temporis filia, the daughter of Tyme. Which two ſo appoynted, went forwarde, toward the South ſyde of the pageant. And on her breſt was written her propre name, whiche was Veritas.

The receiuing

Veritas. Trueth who helde a booke in her hande vpon the which was written, Verbum veritatis, the woorde of trueth. And out of the South syde of the pageaunt was cast a standynge for a chylde which should enterpret thesame pageant. Against whome, when the Quenes maiestie came: he spake vnto her grace these woordes.

This olde man with the sythe, old father tyme they call,
And her his daughter Truth, whiche holdeth yonder boke
Whom he out of this rocke hath brought furth to vs all,
Fro whence this many yeres she durst not once out loke.

The ruthfull wight that sitteth vnder the barren tree,
Resembleth to vs the fourme, when comon weales decay.
But when they be in state tryumphant, you may see
By him in freshe attyre that sitteth vnder the baye.

Now sice ẏ Time agai his daughter truth hath brought,
We trust O worthy quene, thou wilt this truth embrace.
And since thou vnderstandst the good estate and nought
We trust welth thou wilt plant, and barrennes displace.

But for to heale the sore, and cure that is not seene,
Which thing ẏ boke of truth doth teache in writig plain:
She doth present to thee thesame, O worthy Queene,
For that, that wordes do flye, but wryting doth remayn.

When the childe had thus ended his speache, he reached hys boke towardes the Quenes maiestie, which a little before, Trueth had let downe vnto him from the hill, whiche by maister Parrat was receiued, and deliuered vnto the Quene. But she as soone as she had receiued the booke, kyssed it, and with both her handes held vp thesame, and so laid it vpon her brest, with great thankes to the citie ther-

of the Queenes maiestie.

tie therfore. And so wēt forward towards Paules churchyarde. The former matter which was rehersed vnto the Queenes maiestie was written in two tables, on either side the pageant eight verses, and in the middest, these in laten.

Ille, vides falcem læua qui sustinet vncam,
  Tempus is est, cui stat filia vera comes
Hanc pater exesa deductam rupe reponit
  In lucem, quam non viderat ante diu
Qui sedet a læua cultu male tristis inepto
  Quem duris crescens cautibus orbis obit
Nos monet effigie, qua sit respublica quando
  Corruit, at contra quando beata viget.
Ille docet iuuenis forma spectandus amictu
  Scitus, et æterna laurea fronde virens.

The sentences written in latin and englishe vpon both the trees, declaring the causes of both estates, were these.

⸿ Causes of a ruinous common weale
are these.

VVāt of the feare of god.   *Blindnes of guides.*
Disobedience to rulers.   *Briberie in maiestrats*
            D.i.   *Rebellion*

The receiuing

Rebellion in subiectes.   Vnmercifullnes in rulers.
Ciuill disagrement.   Vnthākfulnes in subiectes
Flattring of princes.

⁋ **Causes of a flozishing common weale.**

Feare of god.   Obedient subiectes.
A wise prince.   Louers of the cōmon weale
Learned rulers.   Vertue rewarded
Obedience to officers.   Vice chastened.

The mater of this pageāt depēdeth of them ƥ went befoze. For as the first declared her grace to cōe out of ƥ house of vnitie, ƥ second ƥ she is placed in ƥ seate of gouernment staied with vertues to the suppzessiō of vice, and therfoze in the third the eight blessinges of almighty god might well be applied vnto her: so this fourth now is, to put her grace in remembzāce of the state of the common weale, which Time with Truth his doughter doth reuele, which Truth also her grace hath receiued, & therfoze cānot but be merciful & careful foz the good gouernment therof. Frō thence the Quenes maiesty passed toward Paules churchyard And whē she came ouer agaist Paules scole, a childe appointed by ƥ scolemaster therof pronounced a certein ozacion in latin, & certain verses, which also wer there wzitten as foloweth.

Philosophus ille diuinus Plato inter multa preclare ac sapienter dicta, hoc posteris proditū reliquit, Rempub: illā fælicissimā fore, cui priceps sophiæ studiosa, virtutibusq, ornata cōtigerit. Quem si vere

of the Queenes maiestie.

si vere dixisse censeamus (vt quidē verissime) cur nō terra Britānica plauderet? cur nō populus gaudiū atq̃ lætitiā agitaret? immo, cur nō hunc diē albo (quod aiunt) lapillo notaret? quo princeps talis nobis adest, qualē priores nō viderūt, qualēq̃ posteritas haud facile cernere poterit, dotibᵒ quū animi, tū corporis vndiq̃ fæcilicissima. Casti quidem corporis dotes ita apertæ sūt, vt oratione nō egeant. Animi vero tot tātæq̃, vt ne verbis quidē exprimi possint. Hæc nēpe Regibᵒ sūmis orta, morū atq̃ animi nobilitate genus exuperat. Huius pectᵒ Cristi religionis amore flagrat. Hæc gentē Britannicā virtutibus illustrabit, clipeoq̃ iustitiæ teget. Hæc literis græcis et latinis eximia, ingenioq̃ prepollēs est. Hac imperante pietas vigebit, Anglia florebit, aurea secula redibūt. Vos igitur Angli tot cōmoda accepturi Elizabethā Reginā nostrā celeberrimā ab ipso Christo huiᵘ regni imperio destinatā, honore debito prosequimini. Huiᵘ imperiis aio libētissimo subditi estote, vos q̃ tali pricipᵉ dignos prebete. Et quoniā pueri nō viribᵒ sed precibᵒ officiū prestare possunt, nos Alumni huius scholæ ab ipso Coleto olim Templi Paulini Decano, extructæ, teneras palmas ad cælum tendentes Christū Opt: Maxi: precaturi sumus vt tuā celsitudinem annos Nestoreos summo cum honore Anglis imperitare faciat, matremq̃ pignoribus charis beatam reddat. Amen.

D.ii. Anglia

The receiuing

Anglia nunc tandem plaudas, lætare, resulta,
  Presto iam vita est, præsidiumq́, tibi
En tua spes venit tua gloria, lux, decus omne
  Venit iam solidam quæ tibi prestat opem.
Succurretq́, tuis rebus quæ pessum abiere.
  Perdita quæ fuerant hæc reparare volet
Omnia florebunt, redeunt nunc aurea secla.
  In melius surgent quæ cecidere bona.
Debes ergo illi totam te reddere fidam
  Cuius in accessu commoda tot capies.
Salue igitur dicas, imo de pectore summo.
  Elizabeth Regni non dubitanda salus,
Virgo venit, veniatq́, optes comitata deinceps.
  Pignoribus charis, læta parens veniat
Hoc deus omnipotens ex alto donet olympo
  Qui cælum & terram condidit atq́, regit.

Which the Queenes maiestie most attentiuely harkened vnto. And when the childe had pronounced he did kisse the oration which he had there faire written in paper, and deliuered it vnto the Quenes maiestie, which most gētly receiued the same. And when the Quenes maiestie had heard all y̑ was there offred to be spokē, thē her grace marched toward Ludgate where she was receiued with a noyse of instrumētes, the forefront of y̑ gate being finelie trimmed vp against her maiesties cōming.
                                                     From

of the Queenes maieſtie.

From thence by the way as ſhe went down toward Fletebridge, one aboute her grace noted the cities charge, that there was no coaſt ſpared. Her grace anſwered that ſhe did well conſider the ſame, and that it ſhould be remembred. An honorable anſwere, worthie a noble prince, which may comfort all her ſubiectes, conſidering there can be no point of gentlenes, or obedient loue ſhewed towarde her grace, which ſhe doth not moſt tenderlie accept, and graciouſly waye. In this maner, the people on either ſide reioyſing, her grace went forwarde, towarde the conduite in Fleeteſtrete, where was the fift, and laſte pageant erected in forme folowing. From the conduit which was bewtiſied with painting, vnto the Northſide of the ſtrete, was erected a ſtage embattelled with foure towres and in the ſame a ſquare platte riſing with degrees, and vpon the vppermoſt degree was placed a chaire, or ſeate roiall, and behinde the ſame ſeate in curious, artificiall maner was erected a tre of reaſonable height and ſo farre aduaunced aboue the ſeate as it did well and ſemely ſhadow the ſame, without endomaging the ſight of any part of the pageant, and the ſame tree was bewtiſied with leaues as grene as arte could deuiſe, being of a conuenient greatnes and conteining therupon the fruite of the date, and on the top of the ſame tree in a table was ſet the name therof which was A Palme tree, and in the aforeſaid ſeate or chaire was placed a ſemelie and mete perſonage

D.iii. rich-

The receiuing

richlie apparelled in parliament robes, with a sceptre in her hand, as a Queene, crowned with an open
crowne, whose name and title was in a table fixed
ouer her head, in this sort. Debora the iudge and
restorer of the house of Israel. Iudic. 4. and the
other degrees on eyther side were furnished wyth
vi. personages, two representing the nobilitie, two ye
clergie, & two the cōminaltie. And before these personages was written in a table Debora with her
estates, consulting for the good gouernment of Israel. At the feete of these and the lowest part of the
pageant was ordeined a conuenient rome for a
childe to open the meaning of the pageant. When
the Queenes maiestie drew nere vnto this pageāt,
and perceiued, as in the other, the childe readie to
speake, her grace required silēce, and commaunded
her chariot to be remoued nigher, that she might
plainlie heare the childe speake, which said as hereafter foloweth.

Iaben of Canaan king had long by force of armes
Opprest the Israelites, which for gods people went
But god minding at last for to redresse their harmes,
The worthy Debora as iudge among them sent.

In war she, through gods aide, did put her foes to flight,
And with the dint of sworde the bande of bondage brast.
In peace she, through gods aide, did alway maintcine
And iudged Israell till fourty yeres were past. (right

A worthie president, O worthie Queene, thou hast,
A worthie woman iudge, a woman sent for state.
And that the like to vs endure alway thou maist
Thy louing subiectes wil w true hearts & tonges praie.

which

of the Queenes maiestie.

Which verses were written vpon the pageant, and the same in latin also.

Quando dei populum Canaan, rex preſſit Iaben,
  Mittitur a magno Debora magna deo:
Quæ populum eriperet, ſanctum ſeruaret Iudan,
  Milite quæ patrio frangeret hoſtis opes.
Hæc domino mandante deo lectiſſima fecit
  Fæmina, et aduerſos contudit enſe viros.
Hæc quater denos populum correxerat annos
  Iudicio, bello ſtrenua, pace grauis.
Sic, O ſic populum belloq́ et pace guberna,
  Debora ſis Anglis Elizabetha tuis.

The voide places of the pageant were filled with pretie ſentēces concerning the same matter. The ground of this laſt pageant was, p̄ forſomuch as the next pageant before had ſet before her graces eyes the floriſhing & deſolate ſtates of a cōmon weale, ſhe might by this be put in remēbrance to cōſult for the worthie gouernmēt of of her people, conſidering god oftimes ſent women nobly to rule among men, as Debora which gouerned Iſraell in peace the ſpace of xl. yeres: & that it behoueth both men & women ſo ruling to vſe aduiſe of good counſell. When p̄ Queenes maieſtie had paſſed this pageāt, ſhe marched towarde Tēple barre. But at S. Dunſtones church where the childrē of thoſpitall wer appointed to ſtāde with their gouernours, her grace perceiuig

D.iiii.　　　　　a childe

The receiuing

a childe offred to make an oracion vnto her, staied her chariot, and did cast vp her eyes to heauen, as who shoulde saye, I here see this mercifull worke towarde the poore whom I must in the middest of my royaltie nedes remembre, and so turned her face towarde the childe, which in latin pronounced an oracion to this effecte, that after the Queenes highnes had passed through the citie and had sene so sumpteous, rich, and notable spectacles of the citiezens which delared their most hartye receyuing and ioyous welcomming of her grace into the same: thys one spectacle yet rested and remained, which was the euerlasting spectacle of mercy vnto the poore members of allmighty God, furthered by that famous and most noble prince king Henry the eyght, her graces father, erected by the citie of London, and aduaunced by the most godly verteous and gracious prince king Edwarde the .vi. her graces dere and louing brother doubting nothing of the mercy of the Queenes most gracious clemencie by the which they may not onely be releued and helped, but also stayed and defended, & therfore incessautly they would pray and crie vnto almighty god for the long life and raigne of her highnes with most prosperous victory against her enemies.

 The childe after he had ended his oracion, kissed the paper wherin the same was written, and reached it to the Queenes maiestie which receiued it graci-

of the Quenes maiestie.

graciouslye both with woordes & countenance, declaring her gracious mynde toward their reliefe. From thence her grace came to Temple barre, whiche was dressed finely with the two ymages of Gotmagot the Albione, and Corineus the Briton, two gyātes bigge in stature furnished accordingly, which held in their hādes euē aboue ỹ gate, a table, wherin was writen in laten verses, the effect of al the pageantes which the citie before had erected, which verses wer these.

Ecce sub aspectu iam contemplaberis vno
   O princeps populi sola columna tui.
Quicquid in immensa passim perspexeris vrbe
   Quæ cepere omnes vnus hic arcus habet.
Primus te solio regni donauit auiti,
   Hæres quippe tui vera parentis eras.
Suppressis vitiis, domina virtute, Secundus
   Firmauit sedem regia virgo tuam.
Tertius ex omni posuit te parte beatam
   Si, qua cæpisti pergere velle, velis.
Quarto quid verum, respublica lapsa quid esset
   Quæ florens staret te docuere tui.
Quinto magna loco monuit te Debora, missam
   Cælitus in regni gaudia longa tui.
Perge ergo regina, tuæ spes vnica gentis,
   Hæc postrema vrbis suscipe vota tuæ.

                     E.j.   *Viue*

The receiuing

Viue diu, regnaq̃, diu, virtutibus orna
  Rem patriam, et populi spem tueare tui.
Sic o sic petitur cælum Sic itur in astra
  Hoc virtutis opus, cætera mortis erunt.

Which verses wer also written in Englishe meter in a lesse table as herafter foloweth.

Behold here in one view, thou mayst see all that plaine
O princesse to this thy people the onely staye:
What echewhere thou hast seen in this wide town, again
This one arche whatsoeuer the rest conteynd, doth say.

The first arche as true heyre vnto thy father dere,
Did set thee in the throne where thy graund father satte,
The second dyd confyrme thy seate as princesse here,
Uertues now bearyng swaye, and vices bet down flatts.

The third, if that thou wouldest goe on as thou began,
Declared thee to be blessed on euery side,
The fourth did open Trueth, and also taught thee whan
The commō weale stoode well, & when it did thence slide.

The fifth as Debora declared thee to be sent
From heauen, a long comfort to vs thy subiectes all,
Therfore goe on O Queene, on whom our hope is bent,
And take with thee this wishe of thy towne as finall,

Liue long, and as long raigne, adourning thy countrie,
With vertues, and maintain thy peoples hope of thee,
For thus, thus heauē is won, thus must ỹ pearce ỹ skye,
This is by vertue wrought, all other must nedes dye.

On the South side was appointed by the citie a noyse of singing children, & one child richely attyred as a Poet, which gaue the quenes maiestie her farewel in ỹ name of the hole citie, by these wordes.

As at thine entraunce first, O prince of high renowne,
                                                      Thou

of the Quenes maiestie.

Thou wast preseted with tonges & heartes for thy fayre,
So now sith thou must nedes depart out of this towne
This citie sendeth thee firme hope and earnest praier.,

For all men hope in thee, that all vertues shall reygne,
For all men hope that thou, none errour wilt support,
For all men hope that thou wilt trueth restore agayne,
And mend that is amisse, to all good mennes comfort.

And for this hope they pray, thou mayst continue long,
Our Quene amongst vs here, all vice for to supplant,
And for this hope they pray y^t God may make the strong
As by his grace puissant, so in his trueth constant.

Farewell O worthy Quene, and as our hope is sure,
That into errours place, thou wilt now trueth restore,
So trust we y^t thou wilt our soueraigne Quene endure,
And louing Lady stand, from hencefurth euermore.

 While these wordes were in saieng, and certeine wisshes therein repeted for maintenaunce of truthe and rooting out of errour she now and then helde vp her handes to heauen warde and willed the people to say. Amen.

 When the childe had ended, she sayd, be ye well assured, I will stande your good quene. At which saieng her grace departed forth through teple barre towarde Westminster with no lesse shooting and crieng of the people, then she entred the citie with a noyse of ordinance which the towre shot of at her graces entraunce first into towre streat.

 The childes saieng was also in latin verses written in a table which was hanged vp there.

O Regina potēs, quum primā vrbem ingredereris
Dona tibi, linguas fidaq̃ corda dedit

      E.ii.   Disce-

The receiuing

Discedenti etiam tibi nunc duo munera mittit.
  Omina plena spei, votaq́ plena precum.
Quippe tuis spes est, in te quod prouida virtus
  Rexerit, errori nec locus vllus erit.
Quippe tuis spes est, quod tu verum omne reduces
  Solatura bonas, dum mala tollis, opes.
Hac spe freti orant, longum vt Regina gubernes,
  Et regni excindas crimina cuncta tui.
Hac spe freti orant, diuina vt gratia fortem,
  Et veræ fidei te velit esse basin.
Iam Regina vale, et sicut nos spes tenet vna,
  Quod vero inducto, perditus error erit.
Sic quoq́ speramus quod eris Regina benigna
  Nobis per regni tempora longa tui.

Thus the Queenes hyghnesse passed through the citie, whiche without anye forreyne persone, of it selfe beautifyed it selfe, and receiued her grace at all places as hath been before mencioned, with most tender obedience and loue, due to so gracious a quene and soueraigne ladie. And her grace likewise of her syde in all her graces passage shewed her selfe generallye an ymage of a woorthie Ladie and Gouernour, but priuately these especiall poyntes were noted in her grace, as signes of a most prince lyke courage, whereby her louing subiectes maye ground a sure hope for the rest of her gracious doinges herafter.

❡ Certeyn

of the Quenes maieſtie.

Certain notes of the quenes maiesties great mercie, clemencie, and wisdom vsed iu this passage

Aboute the nether ende of Cornehill towarde Cheape, one of the knightes about her grace had espyed an auncient citizen, which wepte, and turned his head backe, and therwith said this gentleman, yonder is an Alderman (for so he tearmed hym) which wepeth & turneth his face backeward. How may it be interpreted that he so doth, for sorowe, or for gladnes? The quenes maiestie hearde him, and said, I warrant you it is for gladnes. A gracious interpretatiō of a noble courage, which wold turne the doutefull to the beſt. And yet it was well known that as her grace did confirme the same, the parties cheare was moued for very pure gladnes for the sight of her maiesties person, at ye beholding wherof, he tooke such comfort that with teares he expreſſed the same.

In Cheapeside her grace smyled, and being therof demaunded the cause, answered, for that she had heard one say, Remember old king Henry theight. A naturall child, which at the verie remēbraūce of her fathers name toke so great a ioy, ye all men may well thinke, that as she reioysed at his name whom this realme doth holde of so woorthie memorie: so in her doinges she will resemble the same.

When the cities charge withoute parcialitie, and onely the citie was mencioned vnto her grace, She sayd it shoulde not be forgotten. Which saying might moue al natural Englishmen hertely to shew
                     E.iii.   due

The receiuing

due obedience and entiernes to their, so good a Queene which will in no point forget anie parcell of duetie louinglie shewed vnto her.

The answere which her grace made vnto maister Recorder of London, as the hearers know it to be true, and with melting heartes herd the same: so may the reader therof conceiue what kinde of stomacke and courage pronounced the same.

What more famous thing doe we reade in auncient histories of olde time, then that mightye princes haue gentlie receiued presentes offered them by base and low personages. If that be to be wondered at (as it is passingly) let me se any writer that in any one princes life is able to recount so manie presidentes of this virtue, as her grace shewed in ẏ one passage through the citie. How many nosegaies did her grace receiue at poore womens handes? how ofttimes staied she her chariot, when she saw any simple body offer to speake to her grace? A brãche of Rosemarie giuen to her grace with a supplicatiõ by a poore woman about fleetebridge, was sene in her chariot till her grace came to westminster, not without the meruaillous wondring of such as knew the presenter and noted the Queenes most gracious receiuing and keping the same.

What hope the poore and nedie may looke for at her graces hande, she as in all her iourney continuallie, so her harkening to the poore childrẽ of Christes hospitall with eyes cast vp into heauen, did fullie declare, as that neither the welthier estate

of the Quenes maieſtie.

tate could ſtande without conſideracion had to the pouertie, neither the pouertie be dewlie conſidered, vnles they were remembꝛed, as commended to vs by goddes owne mouth.

As at her firſt enterance ſhe as it were declared, her ſelfe pꝛepared to paſſe thꝛough a citie that moſt entierlie loued her, ſo ſhe at her laſt departing, as it were bownd her ſelfe by pꝛomes to continue good ladie and gouernoꝛ vnto that citie which by outward declaracion did open their loue, to their ſo louing and noble pꝛince in ſuch wiſe, as ſhe her ſelfe wonderyd therat.

But becauſe pꝛinces be ſet in their ſcate by gods appointing and therfoꝛe they muſt firſt and chiefſlie tēder the gloꝛy of him, from whom their gloꝛie iſſueth, it is to be noted in her grace, that foꝛſomuch as god hath ſo wonderfullie placed her in the ſeate of gouernment ouer this realme, ſhe in all doinges doth ſhew her ſelfe moſt mindfull of his goodnes and mercie ſhewed vnto her, & amongeſt all other. two pꝛincipall ſygnes thereof were noted in this paſſage. Firſt in the Towꝛe, where her grace befoꝛe ſhe entred her chariot, lifted vp her eyes to heauen and ſayd.

O Loꝛd, almighty and euerlaſting God, I geue thee moſt heartie thākes that thou haſt been ſo mercifull vnto me as to ſpare me to beholde this ioyfull daye. And I acknowledge that thou haſt dealt as wonderfully & as mercifully with me, as thou didſt

E.iiii.   wyth

The receiuing

with thy true and faithfull seruant Daniel thy prophete whom thou deliueredst out of the denne from the crueltie of the gredy and rageing Lyons: euen so was I ouerwhelmed, and only by thee deliuered. To thee therfore only be thankes, honor, & prayse, for euer. Amen.

The second was the receiuing of ẏ Bible at the little conduit in cheape. For when her grace had learned that the bible in Englishe should there be offered, she thanked the citie therefore, promysed the reading therof most diligentlie, and incontinent commaunded, that it shoulde be brought. At the receit wherof, how reuerently did she with both her handes take it, kisse it, & lay it vpon her brest: to the great comfort of the lookers on. God will vndoubtedly preserue so worthy a prince, which at hys honor so reuerently taketh her beginning. For this saying is true, and written in the boke of Truth. He that first seketh the kingdome of God, shall haue all other thinges cast vnto him.

Now therfore all English hertes, and her naturall people must nedes prayse Gods mercie which hath sent them so woorthie a prince, and pray for her graces long continuance amongest vs.

Imprinted at London in fletestrete within Temple barre, at the signe of the hand and starre, by Richard Tottill, the xxiii. day of January.

*T*HE QUEEN'S ROUTE—certain after Fenchurch, presumed up to that point—is shown on a portion of the map of London printed in Braun and Hogenberg's *Civitates Orbis Terrarum*, Vol. 1, 1612. The map was actually drawn about the time of Elizabeth's accession, for it shows a pointed spire on St. Paul's Cathedral that was destroyed by lightning in 1561 and never rebuilt.

1. Fenchurch, where the Queen received the first formal greeting from the City: an oration in English verse by a child (*page 29*)

2. The upper end of Gracious or Gracechurch Street, where the first pageant was erected (*page 31*)

3. The "nether ende" of Cornhill, the site of the second pageant (*page 37*)

4. Soper's Lane end, just beyond the Great Conduit in Cheapside, where the third pageant was located (*page 41*)

5. The Little Conduit in Cheapside, near which the City presented a thousand marks in gold to the Queen, and where the fourth pageant was erected (*page 44*)

6. St. Paul's School, the Churchyard, where a child delivered an oration (*page 50*)

7. Ludgate, where the Queen was greeted with "a noyse of instrumentes." Here she left the City proper (*page 52*)

8. The Conduit in Fleet Street, where the fifth pageant was erected (*page 53*)

9. Temple Bar, where stood giant images of Gogmagog and Corineus (*page 57*)

Reproduced from a copy in the Map Collection of the Yale University Library.